I0440802

Introduction

Thank you kindly for purchasing *In Your Own Back Yard Children's book* (the 1st in a Series). I thank you from the bottom of my heart for helping me to make in a difference in other's lives.

My main focus for this book (and the others following this) is to make a difference. It is something I am driven to do and my books is a way I know I can accomplish that. My sincere thanks to all of you who will help me achieve my dream and if you have a moment to leave a positive review, bless you!

> *20% of the proceeds are going to be donated to the Cancer Society as that is what ended up taking my dad's life this past November 25th, 2012 and there are so many brave little souls battling this disease who need help.*

It is amazing to look at the world through a child's eyes. They find everything so amazing, wondrous, interesting...and as adults we tend to misplace that enthusiasm they have for life. Through my photography, I find myself in awe of everything around me. From the trees to the wildlife in my own back yard and on my drives to the nearest big town (I live in a small rural municipality), I take my camera to capture something new on my journey.

That is why I decided to create this series, "In Your Own Back Yard." From bugs to birds, flowers to trees, we will discover what we usually take for granted...and perhaps we all can learn something new along the way!

Dedication

This book is first dedicated to God. Thank you for all your blessings & favours.

This is also dedicated to my husband Michael and my fur babies (Keysha, Blue, Tess, Shamrock and Gabrielle). Thank you for your love, strength and support, I truly couldn't have made it without you.

In remembrance of my dad who passed away in November. Dad I love & miss you terribly.
Thank you for giving me your artistic talent, your encouragement and support for everything I did. There isn't a day that goes by I don't think of you.

Table of Contents

Bumble Bee

Bumblebees have black and yellow stripes.

You may hear a bumblebee's familiar buzzing before you see it.

Bumblebees fly from flower to flower, drinking the sweet nectar and spreading pollen.

Spreading pollen from plant to plant is very important.

Because without it plants could not grow more flowers or fruits.

They shake a flower, causing the pollen to drop.

This is called buzz pollination.

Bees use this to catch some of the pollen and later eat it!

If you want some beautiful flowers, invite a bumblebee into your backyard.

And don't worry, while bumblebees can sting; they won't if they are left alone to gather nectar and pollen.

Bumblebees usually build their nest near or under the ground, including underground tunnels, bushy clumps of grass, or even seat cushions left outside.

13 Banded Ground Squirrel

The 13 lined or banded ground squirrel is named for the thirteen stripes running down its tiny beige back.

The stripes are dark and light colored with yellowish dots on the stripes.

For a squirrel that is less than 12 inches long and weighs less than a ½ can of soda pop, it is certainly pretty to look at, if you can find it.

It can be hard to find because the lines on the squirrel help it with camouflage.

It allows the squirrel to safely run through the meadows and tall grassy areas without being seen.

This squirrel lives in burrows under the ground.

At night, the squirrel closes off the entrances with a clod of dirt or grass to keep predators out.

In winter they hibernate in burrows where their heart beat will slow down from 200 to 20 beats a minute!

When they dig out in early spring, the squirrels will look for seeds, flowers, insects, lizards, and mice to eat.

They will even eat bird eggs and baby birds if they can find them!

Monarch Butterfly

Did you know that monarch butterflies are poisonous?

The monarch's color pattern of orange and black lets enemies know that it will taste bad and make them sick.

Some birds, like the Baltimore Orioles and Grosbeaks have figured out ways to eat the butterfly and not get sick.

When they're caterpillars, they eat milkweed, a plant that contains a toxin or poison.

The toxin doesn't hurt the caterpillar, but it can make other animals sick.

The caterpillar stores up the toxin, and when it becomes a butterfly, it is still poisonous.

Because of this, most predators that eat butterflies and caterpillars, such as birds and insects, avoid the monarch butterfly!

They feed on the nectar of flowers.

Butterflies are quick learners.

They prefer yellow flowers, but they learn to go to flowers that have the most nectar, even if they aren't yellow.

The butterflies even remember this information for up to 3 days! What smart butterflies!

Robin

The American Robin is a common bird all throughout the United States and the world.

It can be found in almost all regions and is easily identified by its reddish-orange rounded belly and its cheery song.

Robin eggs are a blue-green color.

Some scientists believe that one of the reasons for the color may be to encourage the male robins to care for the baby birds.

A blue-green egg tells a male Robin that this is a good egg and worth taking care of.

Robins also recognize their own eggs.

Robins like to eat earthworms and insects.

But did you know that they also like to eat fruit, like:
- hawthorn berries,
- chokecherries,
- and juniper berries?

They like to eat different food at different times of the day, too. For breakfast, they eat mainly worms and insects.

They also eat more fruit in the winter. Robins may even eat fruit that have insects in them, to get a well-rounded meal!

Robins enjoy having a place where they can get together, have a drink and bath on hot summer days.

Honey Bee!

Honeybees are one of the most studied insects.

Honeybees have five hairy eyes, and they never sleep. Ever!

Honeybees have been around for about 100 million years.

Fossils of bees were found from 40 million years ago!

Farmers depend on a honeybee's ability to spread pollen between plants in order to have a good harvest.

One of the jobs for a worker bee is to fly from flower to flower and collect nectar and pollen on their hind legs.

They bring this back to the nest to feed the colony.

There are three kinds of honeybees in a nest or colony:

1. the queen bee,

2. the drones,

3. and the worker bees.

There is only one queen bee, and she is responsible for laying all the eggs that will become the new bees.

The drones are male bees; there may be a few hundred of them in a hive.

Squirrel

You probably know a lot about squirrels.

You've probably seen them running through the grass, darting across a road, or scampering up a tree.

You may have heard them chattering to one another or scolding a person for getting too close.

Did you know that there are over 200 species, or types, of squirrels in the world?

There are tree squirrels, ground squirrels and even flying squirrels.

Tiger Salamander

Tiger salamanders are amphibians, and they have a variety of skin coloring.

A lot of these salamanders are dark brown or black with yellow stripes covering their body, but some have a green or gray body with dots instead of stripes.

Tiger salamanders live a long time, from 10 – 16 years.

As adults, they live in burrows underground and only come out at night to hunt.

They are carnivores, which mean they eat meat, like frogs, worms, and insects.

If a tiger salamander tangles with another animal and loses one of its legs or its tail, that's no problem. It will just grow another one!

Tiger salamanders, as well as other kinds of salamanders, are even able to regrow, or regenerate, parts of their spinal cord or brain!

Tiger salamanders start their lives in a pond or body of water.

They hatch from eggs as larvae and stay there for a few months before fully developing into an adult salamander.

If the land is too dry, however, the tiger salamander may just live forever in the water.

The Fly

Flies are everywhere!

There are over 120, 000 different species or types of flies in the world.

Most flies are considered pests as they are not very clean.

A fly can have up to 2 million bacteria on its body at one time and they carry over 100 different disease causing germs!

They go to the bathroom every 4-5 minutes and they don't use a bathroom!

Flies love garbage. One trash bin, if not emptied can allow 1000 flies to hatch and grow per week!

Have you noticed that flies can walk on walls and ceilings without falling?

Their sticky feet allow them to stick to any surface!

Did you know that flies have eyes that are made up of hundreds of thousands of tiny little lens's?

These allow them to see a larger space around them and detect even the slightest movement!

It's like having a 360 degree view of your surroundings!

It eats garbage scraps, pet poop, and any decaying, or rotting, thing. Yuck!

In Conclusion… **Thank you for taking the time to read this book!**

"No matter how big or small, acts of kindness are never wasted. With every gesture, with every step we can all make a difference in someone's life."

If you have the time to leave a positive review, it would be most gratefully appreciated.

Thank you kindly…God Bless.

Please check out my other book for Charity:

Traditional Old English Recipes

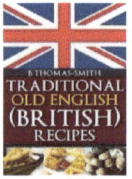

http://www.amazon.com/Traditional-Old-English-British-Recipes-ebook/dp/B00BCUJHL0/ref=zg_bs_156222011_10

www.ingramcontent.com/pod-product-compliance
Lightning Source LLC
Chambersburg PA
CBHW050859290526
45792CB00002B/655